LIVING WITH
PANIC
DISORDER

by Jennifer Connor-Smith

ReferencePoint
Press®

San Diego, CA

© 2019 ReferencePoint Press, Inc.
Printed in the United States

For more information, contact:
ReferencePoint Press, Inc.
PO Box 27779
San Diego, CA 92198
www.ReferencePointPress.com

LIBRARY OF CONGRESS CATALOGING-IN-PUBLICATION DATA

Name: Connor-Smith, Jennifer, 1972– author.
Title: Living with Panic Disorder / by Jennifer Connor-Smith, PhD.
Description: San Diego, CA : ReferencePoint Press, Inc., [2019] | Series:
    Living with Disorders and Disabilities | Audience: Grade 9 to 12. |
    Includes bibliographical references and index.
Identifiers: LCCN 2018011539 (print) | LCCN 2018011761 (ebook) | ISBN
    9781682824863 (eBook) | ISBN 9781682824856 (hardback)
Subjects: LCSH: Anxiety—Juvenile literature. | Panic disorders—Juvenile
    literature.
Classification: LCC RC531 (ebook) | LCC RC531 .C664 2019 (print) | DDC
    616.85/22—dc23
LC record available at https://lccn.loc.gov/2018011539

CONTENTS

A MOMENT OF PANIC

Makayla is a sixteen-year-old soccer player and honors student. Or she was, until she quit the team and stopped going to school last month. The problems began with a terrifying episode in her math class. Out of nowhere, Makayla's chest tightened, making it hard to breathe. She became dizzy and faint, and strange tingling sensations filled her arms and legs. Her teacher's voice faded into the background. Everyone around her seemed strangely plastic and unfamiliar. Although the terrifying episode passed, the fear of losing her mind lingered.

The last straw came a week later when Makayla had an episode at lunch. In her disoriented state, she thought she was losing her mind. Everyone around her seemed hollow. She sprinted from the room, hoping to get home before she went completely insane.

Since then, Makayla has stayed home. Her friends have asked to visit, but Makayla refuses, feeling certain she would scare them by acting weird. She continues to have dizzy episodes. Each time, she thinks the symptoms will get worse and worse until she loses contact with reality forever.

Panic disorder can cause a variety of physical symptoms. Panic attacks can be mistaken for dizziness, heart attacks, or other problems.

Eric's Story

Eric is a twenty-five-year-old construction worker who has been on unpaid leave for the last six months due to a series of terrifying cardiac events. In these events, his heart races, pounds, and skips irregularly. He feels crushing chest pain and gasps to get enough air. Sweat pours from his body, his muscles shake, and waves of nausea wash over him.

Eric's first episode happened while he was carrying a heavy load at work. Over the next month, Eric continued to have episodes. During each ambulance ride, he scrawled frantic notes to his wife and two-year-old daughter, telling them he loved them. Although Eric has gone to the emergency room almost 30 times and worked with three different specialists, he remains convinced the doctors have

"It feels like your mind is desperately trying to regain control of a body that has gone completely rogue. The more your mind tries to unscramble the circuits in your head, lungs, and limbs, the more your body tenses, hyperventilates, panics, and fights back."[1]

—Panic attack victim

overlooked a life-threatening condition. He falls asleep each night wondering if he will wake up the next day.

Solving the Mystery

Makayla and Eric's stories are fictional examples of the same problem: panic disorder. In panic disorder, people experience unexpected episodes of extreme fear, called panic attacks. Panic attacks can be so intense that people believe they are dying or going insane. One woman describes her experience by saying, "It feels like your mind is desperately trying to regain control of a body that has gone completely rogue. The more your mind tries to unscramble the circuits in your head, lungs, and limbs, the more your body tenses, hyperventilates, panics, and fights back."[1]

Psychologists Stanley Rachman and Padmal de Silva explain, "On average, episodes of panic last between 10 and 20 minutes, are extremely distressing, and leave the person feeling drained and apprehensive."[2] Although the overwhelming symptoms typically last only a few minutes, the experience is so frightening that some people organize their lives around preventing future episodes. At that point, having panic attacks becomes panic disorder. A formal diagnosis of panic disorder requires "persistent concern or worry about additional panic attacks" or "a significant maladaptive change in behavior related to the attacks," according to the *Diagnostic and Statistical Manual of Mental Disorders* (DSM).[3]

People with panic disorder often fear being humiliated or helpless during a panic attack. To manage that fear, they may avoid places where they have panicked in the past or go out only with a trusted companion. In serious cases, they may develop agoraphobia, a fear of being any place where escape may be difficult or where help may be unavailable. Agoraphobia can be truly devastating, making it impossible to go to school, shop for groceries, or see friends. Psychologist Gordon Asmundson and his colleagues noted, "More than a third of individuals with agoraphobia are unable to leave their homes to work."[4]

> **"More than a third of individuals with agoraphobia are unable to leave their homes to work."[4]**
>
> —*Gordon Asmundson, psychologist*

Fortunately, there are many effective treatments for panic disorder and agoraphobia. Medications can offer rapid relief while people develop the skills to overcome panic. People can learn to see anxiety itself as a tool, rather than something to fear. Psychologist Michael Tompkins explains, "Anxiety pushes us to plan and prepare. Anxiety is evidence of our will to live, to prosper, and to transcend the things that threaten us."[5]

Over the course of a lifetime, about one out of every four people will experience a panic attack. Research suggests that understanding panic attacks can make people less likely to develop panic disorder. Learning about panic disorder may someday help someone you love understand a frightening experience and get help quickly.

Chapter 1

WHAT IS PANIC DISORDER?

Everyone has experienced worry. Chances are, you have felt jittery and nervous before giving a speech. You have probably felt dread about confessing a mistake. Maybe you've suffered a sleepless night worrying about an argument or upcoming test.

But worry and anxiety can be complex. They may be focused on the distant future or an immediate threat. They can range from mild worries to sheer terror. People also differ in how they experience anxiety. Some people can't focus on taking tests because their minds race. Others can think clearly but suffer crushing headaches. Some people are calm in the face of crisis while others react strongly to minor problems.

People suffering from anxiety may have such severe fear that they are unable to leave their beds. They may isolate themselves until their feelings of anxiety pass.

Although people experience anxiety differently, most people find it unpleasant. However, that doesn't mean worry is bad. These emotions are not just normal; they are necessary. These feelings exist to protect us from danger, bad decisions, and poor planning. Without anxiety, people would quickly find themselves in trouble. People with especially low levels of anxiety tend to make poor choices. They drive recklessly, try foolish stunts, or blow off work.

Worry motivates us to study for tests, save money for the future, and think twice before gossiping. Fear keeps us from walking down dark alleys late at night or dashing across busy roadways.

Psychologist Bret Moore says, "[Anxiety] improves physical and mental performance, counters fatigue, and motivates people to do things they would otherwise avoid."[6]

When Does Anxiety Become a Disorder?

Although anxiety helps keep us safe, intense anxiety can cause problems. Nausea and agitation make class presentations harder. Being too keyed up to sleep leaves people groggy and unfocused the next day. Even so, feeling overwhelmed occasionally is normal and common. Experiencing fear, grief, or rage is not the same thing as having a psychological disorder. Feeling devastated after a breakup or panicking about a lost pet is part of being human.

Anxiety becomes a psychological disorder when it starts to take over someone's life. To count as a disorder, anxiety must be unusually intense or long-lasting. It must also cause powerful distress or interfere with a person's ability to work or have fun.

How Do Doctors Diagnose Psychological Disorders?

Diagnosing psychological problems can be tricky. It is not always obvious where to draw the line between typical levels of anxiety and problematic ones. For example, many people scream and feel panicky when they see a nonpoisonous snake. Other people keep snakes as pets. Who decides how much anxiety about a snake is normal? The answer would surely depend on who you ask.

For many medical conditions, doctors have clear diagnostic tests. To diagnose strep throat, they look for a specific strain of bacteria.

If a throat swab reveals that bacteria, then the patient has strep throat. For psychological disorders, there is no clear test. Instead, clinicians gather information about a person's thoughts, feelings, and behaviors. They use their expertise to decide whether their client's experience matches the symptoms of a disorder.

However, clinicians do not make diagnoses based on gut instincts. They must follow a strict set of diagnostic criteria. In the United States, most clinicians make diagnoses using the DSM. The DSM details the type and number of symptoms required for each psychological diagnosis. Mental health experts update the DSM regularly to reflect new research. As of 2018, the DSM-5 is the most current version.

Clinicians diagnose psychological disorders by considering people's thoughts, feelings, and behaviors. However, that does not mean mental health problems are just in people's heads. Psychological disorders have clear biological and environmental causes.

Bailey, a woman who has struggled with anxiety for years, wrote about her experience with panic disorder. She says, "The best thing you can do as a loved one of someone who experiences panic attacks is to recognize it is a real experience. . . . [Panic is] out of the person's control and does not at all affect the person's character or define them as a person."[7]

> "The best thing you can do as a loved one of someone who experiences panic attacks is to recognize it is a real experience. . . . [Panic is] out of the person's control and does not at all affect the person's character or define them as a person."[7]
>
> —Bailey, struggles with anxiety

Perspectives on Panic Attacks across Time and Cultures

The concept of panic attacks has existed around the world for centuries. Records of patients with panic and agoraphobia symptoms date back to ancient Greece. Today, different cultures view panic attacks differently. In Puerto Rico, people may have an *ataque de nervios*, or "attack of nerves." Psychologist Stefan Hofmann has studied cross-cultural expressions of anxiety. He says, "The typical symptoms of an ataque include a sense of impending loss of control, chest tightness, a feeling of heat in the body, palpitations, shaking of the arms and legs, and feelings of imminent fainting." An ataque may also involve screaming, crying, aggression, or self-harm.

In Cambodia, people link pain and disease to the movement of *khyâl* through the body. Khyâl is an air-like substance, sometimes translated as "wind." During khyâl attacks, people have intense neck pain and headaches. They fear the rupture of blood vessels in their necks. These attacks also involve rapid breathing, a pounding heart, blurry vision, dizziness, and ringing ears.

Culture can influence how people understand and experience panic attacks. "Although the DSM-5 addresses some of these issues," says Hofmann, "considerably more research is necessary to understand when and how culture impacts disorders."

Stefan G. Hofmann and Devon E. Hinton, "Cross-Cultural Aspects of Anxiety Disorders," *National Center for Technology Information*, June 2014, www.ncbi.nlm.nih.gov.

What Is the Fight-or-Flight Response?

Imagine being confronted by a hungry bear. You have the same choices as any creature facing a predator. You can fight, flee, or freeze and hope it does not notice you. Although most people rarely face wild animals, our ancestors ran a real risk of becoming a meal. Our bodies remain prepared to respond to life-or-death situations.

In dangerous situations, our bodies activate the fight-or-flight response. The liver releases stored sugar to fuel muscles. Blood flow to muscles increases, and muscles may feel tense or shaky. Heart rate and breathing speed up to make more oxygen available. Sweating increases to cool the body. The brain focuses resources on scanning for threats, creating a sense that time has slowed down. Nonessential functions, such as digestion, are shut down, often causing an upset stomach. This cascade of physical responses prepares the body for rapid action.

Unfortunately, we all have some fight-or-flight reactions when we are perfectly safe. There is often a mismatch between our threat-response system and modern stressors. Our fight-or-flight response kicks in when we meet new people or suddenly realize everyone is handing in a paper we thought was due next week.

In essence, our bodies react to math tests as if they are predators. Our job is to sit calmly and answer the questions. Unfortunately, our bodies have prepared us to dash screaming down the hall or rip the test to shreds.

What Does a Panic Attack Feel Like?

Panic attacks are fight-or-flight reactions that occur when people are not facing any actual risk. Have you ever been in a place with smoke detectors that go off too easily? Some smoke detectors can be set off by a steamy shower or normal cooking. Although there is no risk, the smoke detector blasts the same shrieking warning as it would during a real fire.

Panic attacks are essentially false alarms. The physical changes that could be life-saving in a real emergency simply feel awful without offering any benefit. The DSM-5 defines a panic attack as, "An abrupt surge of intense fear or intense discomfort that reaches a peak within minutes."[8] To count as a panic attack, an episode must involve at least four of the following symptoms:

- A rapid, pounding, or irregular heartbeat

- Sweating

- Trembling or shaking

- Feeling short of breath or smothered

- Choking sensations

- Chest pain or discomfort

- Nausea or an upset stomach

- Feeling dizzy, unsteady, light-headed, or faint

- Chills or heat sensations

- Feelings of numbness or tingling

- Feeling out of touch with reality or disconnected from oneself

- Fear of losing control or "going crazy"

- Fear of dying

Although this list of symptoms defines a panic attack, it does not capture the power of the experience. Consider the following descriptions from three women who have panic attacks.

The first explained, "Panic attacks for me tend to feel more like someone has pushed my head under water, and

> "Panic attacks for me tend to feel more like someone has pushed my head under water, and just when I think I'm going to drown, I'm pulled up for a short breath, only to be pushed back under again."[9]
>
> —Panic attack victim

just when I think I'm going to drown, I'm pulled up for a short breath, only to be pushed back under again."

The second said, "Emotionally, it feels like my brain is crumbling. Physically, it feels like a huge weighted band constricting around my lungs."

The third related, "I begin to feel like my soul is separating from my body. . . . I get tunnel vision and nothing makes sense. I can't talk or understand those talking to me."[9]

The tremendous surge of fear during panic attacks can actually lead people to put themselves at risk. Stanley Rachman and Padmal de Silva explain, "During panics, most people experience a feeling of being trapped, and their overwhelming thought and need is to escape. This powerful urge to flee can lead to impulsive, risky behavior, such as driving too fast or recklessly, or dashing blindly out of a building."[10]

With so many symptoms of panic attacks, panic can take many forms. Consider the very different experiences of Eric and Makayla. Eric's panic attacks involve a pounding heart, sweating, trembling muscles, difficulty breathing, chest pain, and nausea. Given that those are also symptoms of a heart attack,

> "During panics, most people experience a feeling of being trapped, and their overwhelming thought and need is to escape. This powerful urge to flee can lead to impulsive, risky behavior, such as driving too fast or recklessly, or dashing blindly out of a building."[10]
>
> —Stanley Rachman and Padmal de Silva, psychologists

his fear of dying and his many visits to the emergency room are not especially surprising.

Although Makayla also feels chest pressure and has difficulty breathing, the rest of her symptoms are very different. She experiences dizziness, tingling sensations, disorientation, and a sense of disconnection. Given those unusual experiences, it is not surprising that Makayla fears something is wrong with her mind.

What Are the Different Types of Panic Attacks?

Panic attacks may be expected or unexpected. "*Expected panic attacks* are attacks for which there is an obvious cue or trigger,"[11] according to the DSM-5. For example, someone with a long-standing fear of heights might panic while riding to the top of a tall building in a glass elevator.

Panic attacks can also happen out of the blue. According to the DSM-5, "*Unexpected panic attacks* are those for which there is no obvious cue or trigger."[12] For example, a person might have a panic attack while watching a comedy at home or even while sleeping. Panic attacks that wake people from a sound sleep are called nocturnal panic attacks. These nighttime attacks are not caused by bad dreams—they wake people from deep and dreamless sleep. People with frequent nocturnal panic attacks may become afraid to fall asleep. Sleep deprivation can leave them exhausted, making them even more likely to have panic attacks.

Unexpected panic attacks are more distressing than expected attacks, say Rachman and de Silva: "In the absence of any good explanation for the panic, it is virtually impossible to predict when and

Expected panic attacks have an obvious cause. For example, someone with a fear of heights might have a panic attack on a high-ropes course.

where the next episode will occur. The unpredictable and inexplicable qualities of these panics are an added worry and burden. As one cannot be fully assured of being safe at any time or place, it becomes difficult to plan activities."

"Having an occasional episode of panic is common and not a sign of any psychological disorder," say Rachman and de Silva.[13] In any given year, approximately 11 percent of adults in the United States will have a panic attack. Almost one-quarter of people will have a panic attack at some point in their lives. The vast majority of those people will never develop panic disorder.

What Are the Signs of Panic Disorder?

Some people who have panic attacks develop panic disorder. The DSM-5 requires several separate elements for a panic disorder diagnosis.

- A person must have recurrent *unexpected* panic attacks.

- Panic attacks cannot be due to medications, drug use, or medical problems.

- Panic attacks cannot be caused by a different mental disorder, such as post-traumatic stress disorder.

- Panic attacks must lead to an intense fear of panic attacks or significant behavior changes. The fear or behavior changes must last at least one month.

Panic disorder is more about people's reaction to panic attacks than about the attacks themselves. Fear of panic attacks or the consequences of those attacks can leave people drowning in worry. People may completely rearrange their lives in an attempt to avoid panic attacks.

Fear related to panic attacks takes many forms. One of the most common is a fear of death. During panic attacks, many people feel like they are suffocating or having a heart attack. Even after the episode ends, people worry about having a life-threatening condition. Rachman and de Silva point out, "It is perfectly understandable to feel intensely frightened if you believe that you are about to die."[14]

Finding Reliable Information Online

Finding information online about panic disorder is easy. A web search for panic attacks turns up millions of results. Finding accurate information takes more work. Some websites are outdated or muddle the facts. Others sell useless or even harmful treatments. For example, a popular natural remedy for anxiety made from the root of the kava plant can cause liver damage and death.

In general, government agencies, universities, hospitals, and health organizations provide accurate information. To evaluate the reliability of other sources, consider the following questions.

- *Does the information come from experts?* Experts on panic disorder have graduate training in mental health or medicine. They also have experience treating or studying panic attacks.

- *Is the information recent?* Every year, researchers learn more about panic disorder causes and treatments. Avoid outdated websites.

- *Does the source make unreasonable claims?* Some websites promise instant cures. Others claim to have secrets doctors don't want you to know. Panic disorder is treatable, but it takes time and effort. Treatments that sound too good to be true probably are.

- *Is the source objective?* Information should come from the thousands of studies done on panic disorder, not someone's personal opinion. Be especially wary of websites selling a product.

- *Does the source seem accurate?* If a website is full of spelling and grammatical errors, the author may also have been sloppy about facts.

Many people with panic disorder feel paralyzed by concerns about looking "crazy." They fear they will lose control and humiliate themselves in public. Other people see the strange sensations they experience during panic attacks as proof that something is catastrophically wrong with their brains. People with panic disorder may worry that they will eventually fall permanently out of touch with reality.

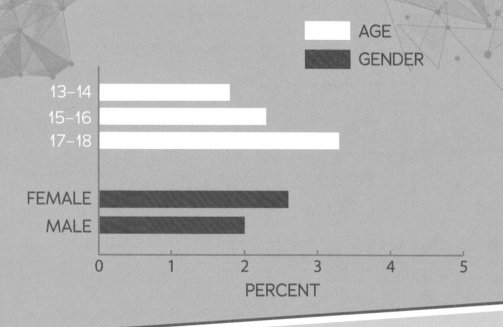

PANIC DISORDER IN TEENS

This graph shows the percentage of teens with panic disorder. As the graph shows, females have a slightly higher risk than males, and older teens have a higher risk than younger teens.

The graph's data comes from the National Institute of Mental Health, one of the National Institutes of Health (NIH). These government research organizations study medical issues in the United States. As part of its mission, the National Institute of Mental Health studies panic disorder. It found that panic disorder has a 2.3 percent lifetime prevalence rate among teenagers. The term *lifetime prevalence* refers to the number of people who had the disorder at any time up until the time when they were surveyed. Anxiety disorders in general, which includes panic disorder, agoraphobia, and social anxiety disorder, affect 31.9 percent of teens.

"Panic Disorder," *National Institute of Mental Health*, n.d. www.nimh.nih.gov.

The examples of Eric and Makayla show how extreme these behavior changes can be. To manage his fear of having a heart attack, Eric has stopped doing anything that raises his heart rate. Unfortunately, his job as a construction worker requires physical labor. Everything from unloading tools to carrying lumber makes his heart beat faster. To protect himself, Eric has stopped going to work. He also stopped working out and going for walks. In an attempt to keep his heart rate steady, he has given up energy drinks, coffee, and soda.

Panic attacks have also caused Makayla to change her behavior. She has no concerns about her physical health but believes she might go insane or act strangely in public. She manages those fears by staying home and avoiding her friends.

What Is Agoraphobia?

Extreme behaviorial changes to deal with panic attacks can lead to agoraphobia. Agoraphobia involves fear of situations that are hard to leave quickly or where help is not available. People with agoraphobia often fear being trapped during a panic attack or medical emergency. Some people with agoraphobia fear humiliating themselves in public. They worry that they may vomit, soil themselves, or act strangely.

For a diagnosis of agoraphobia, people must show extreme fear or avoidance of at least two situations. The avoidance needs to last for about six months. These feared situations must come from the following list:

- Driving or using public transportation

- Being in open spaces, such as a parking lot

- Being in closed spaces, such as a shopping mall or movie theater

- Being in crowded spaces or standing in line

- Being away from home alone

Going to feared spaces may trigger panic attacks or extreme distress. To manage these fears, some people with agoraphobia avoid feared places entirely. Others cannot go out without a trusted friend or family member. The DSM-5 notes, "In its most severe forms, agoraphobia can cause individuals to become completely homebound . . . dependent on others for services or assistance to provide even for basic needs."[15]

Agoraphobia is strongly linked to panic attacks and panic disorder. Virtually all people with agoraphobia experience panic attacks. Approximately 60 percent of people with agoraphobia also have panic disorder.

How Common Are Panic Disorder and Agoraphobia?

In the United States, two to three out of every one hundred teens and adults meet criteria for panic disorder each year. About four to five of every one hundred people will develop panic disorder at some point in their lives. Agoraphobia is less common, with less than two of every one hundred people having agoraphobia at some point in their lives.

Rates of panic disorder are higher for non-Latino whites and American Indians. Rates are lower for Latinos, African Americans, and Asian Americans. Similarly, rates are lower in Latin American, African, and Asian countries.

Females are more likely than males to develop panic disorder or agoraphobia. This sex difference may be due to both biological

People with agoraphobia might avoid places with crowds, such as stadiums or malls. They may worry about the potential for becoming trapped or embarrassed in some way.

and social factors. Men face more social pressure to face their fears directly, which may help prevent agoraphobia. On average they are also more likely to abuse alcohol as a way to manage anxiety.

Panic disorder is relatively rare in children. Only about one out of two hundred children has the disorder. However, many people who develop panic disorder as adults struggled with childhood anxiety. Rates of panic disorder begin to increase during the teen years. About one-half of all people with panic disorder develop the disorder by their early twenties. Without treatment, panic disorder and agoraphobia are likely to persist over time. However, older adults do have lower rates of panic disorder. That might be because the fear response tends to diminish with age. Treatment for panic disorder can help people of all ages.

Chapter 2

WHAT ARE THE EFFECTS OF PANIC DISORDER?

Panic attacks are miserable experiences. But for people with panic disorder, panic attacks may be the least of their issues. Fear leads people to avoid places and activities related to panic attacks. For some people, say Stanley Rachman and Padmal de Silva, "avoidance can become so severe as to shape and limit their entire life. In extreme cases, the person is unable to leave the house except when accompanied, and then only for short distances and brief periods."[16]

Panic disorder can impact every aspect of life, from friendships to work. It is also unlikely to be the only challenge people face.

More than 80 percent of people with panic disorder also have other psychological diagnoses.

What Parts of Life Are Affected by Panic Disorder and Agoraphobia?

Panic disorder leaves no aspect of a person's life untouched. It changes where people go, what they do, and who they see. It may even change what people eat or the movies they watch. Over time, it can damage friendships, destroy self-esteem, and create serious financial problems.

Avoidance is a natural response; we all avoid things that cause pain. Avoidance is also central to panic disorder, as author Rita Chin describes:

> There was a time when basic things—like driving, climbing a flight of stairs, taking a shower, or going through the checkout line at the grocery store—landed me somewhere between mortal unease and full-throttle terror. . . . So I began to avoid things that seemed to trigger my panic attacks—exercise, being in confined spaces, being in open spaces, being in crowds, driving on the highway, etc.—but it didn't matter: My panic would stop at nothing. I even panicked in my sleep.[17]

"So I began to avoid things that seemed to trigger my panic attacks—exercise, being in confined spaces, being in open spaces, being in crowds, driving on the highway, etc.—but it didn't matter: My panic would stop at nothing. I even panicked in my sleep."[17]

—Rita Chin, author

25

Safety Behaviors

Safety behaviors are strategies people use to feel secure in feared situations. Common safety behaviors include:

- standing near exits to make a quick escape possible

- carrying extra medication

- staying near a hospital

- wearing religious symbols

- bringing a friend or pet to feared locations

- tracking the location of family members in case help is required

Safety behaviors can make people less anxious in the short term. But they have a big downside—they can actually increase fear in the long run. People with panic disorder come to believe that they survive only because of their safety behaviors. Psychologists Michelle Craske and David Barlow explain, "Clients may believe that the only reason why they did not die from a panic attack was because they always escaped, avoided, or distracted themselves just in time."

For example, people who feel weak and tingly during panic attacks may cling to objects to prevent passing out. By staying near something to grab, they never learn that they can trust their own legs to hold them up. Instead, they conclude that it is dangerous to be out of reach of a railing. Giving up safety behaviors can be scary, but it brings real benefits. Research shows that when people stop relying on safety behaviors, their anxiety goes down.

Michelle G. Craske and David H. Barlow, *Mastery of Your Anxiety and Panic: Therapist Guide*. Oxford: Oxford University Press, 2007, p. 103.

Some people find panic attacks so excruciating that they avoid anything that produces panic-like sensations. Being sweaty or having their heart beat fast reminds them of panic attacks. Eventually, panic disorder saps the joy from their lives as they give up things they love. People with panic disorder often avoid caffeinated beverages, spicy food, exercise, or other potential triggers.

People with panic disorder also avoid places where they have had panic attacks. Because panic attacks can happen anywhere, the list of places people can't go gets longer and longer. People find their lives getting smaller every day. Eventually, it becomes a struggle just to buy groceries or get to work.

Consider Eric's experience. He had stopped driving because he feared losing control of the car during an episode. But he was determined to buy his wife a birthday present, so he forced himself onto a hot, crowded bus. Eric's anxiety was so high that he was not surprised to find himself gasping for breath and clutching his chest a few minutes later. As his muscles trembled and sweat poured from his forehead, he felt people staring. He jumped off at the next stop and called his mother for a ride home. He felt certain he would have died had he stayed on the bus, and he resolved never to ride a bus again.

Over time, avoidance turns panic attacks into panic disorder. As therapist Jennifer Shannon explains, "Avoidance works so fast and so well, you'll want to use it again. The problem is that with repeated use, avoidance has a nasty side effect: *The more you avoid a situation, the scarier that situation becomes.*"[18]

> "Avoidance works so fast and so well, you'll want to use it again. The problem is that with repeated use, avoidance has a nasty side effect: *The more you avoid a situation, the scarier that situation becomes.*"[18]
>
> —Jennifer Shannon, *therapist*

The short-term benefits of avoidance were already creating high costs for Makayla. The first time Makayla stayed home from school she did not have a dizzy spell.

Panic disorders can make people feel alone. They may avoid their friends and the activities they usually enjoy.

She concluded that staying home kept her safe. But she may well have been panic-free at school too. Believing that home meant safety and school meant danger made Makayla terrified to leave home.

Panic disorder and agoraphobia often lead to financial problems. People may lose wages or quit jobs because anxiety makes it impossible to get to work. Panic attacks can also lead to high medical costs. During panic attacks, people often visit the emergency room, thinking they are in danger of dying or going insane. Emergency room visits plus follow-up appointments with specialists get expensive.

The financial costs of panic disorder have been life-changing for Eric. He has adult responsibilities, like paying a mortgage and bills. Although his wife is now working overtime, her extra work still doesn't cover their expenses. Eric can't even bear to look at the stack of unpaid medical bills. To make matters worse, even though Eric is not working, the family still pays for daycare. Eric is home all day but too afraid to be alone with his daughter.

Panic disorder can damage friendships and cause social isolation. Psychologist Debra Kissen suffered from panic disorder during her teen years. She says, "Panic has a way of robbing you of your sense of connection. Panic may tell you that you are the only one who struggles with strange and uncomfortable thoughts and feelings. It may tell you that no one could possibly understand how you feel."[19]

People who panic often feel self-conscious. They may avoid seeing friends and meeting new people because they fear being judged. Even when they want to see friends, the long list of places and activities they feel compelled to avoid makes it tricky to meet up. People with panic disorder may also worry about leaning too heavily on friends and family. They don't want to wear people down by asking for too much help.

Before panic disorder struck, Makayla had many friends. But a month of skipping school and soccer practice has changed things. Although she has stayed in touch using social media, she hasn't seen anyone in weeks. Looking at pictures of her friends having fun without her makes her feel like a miserable loser. People have already stopped asking her to hang out. Group messages are full of new inside jokes she doesn't get. Makayla feels like everyone is moving on without her.

Eric also feels isolated. Most of his friends are people he knows from work. Outside of work, they used to hike, play basketball, and go on runs. Since Eric no longer exercises, he hasn't seen anyone since he went on leave.

Over time, the onslaught of panic attacks can rob people of their self-esteem and sense of self-worth. People may feel embarrassed about their symptoms or ashamed about the way fear has taken over their lives. Kissen wrote about her own teenage experience, saying, "One painful side effect of my undetected panic disorder was that I came to believe there was something wrong with me. It seemed to me that in some core way I was broken or lacking, and that was why I was experiencing such disturbing sensations."[20]

Panic disorder has rattled Makayla's confidence. She had planned to apply to top colleges after high school. But now those plans are in jeopardy. Her grades have dropped, and she has started to doubt whether she was ever college material. In fact, she isn't sure she will ever be able to move out of her parents' house. She has started to have visions of herself as a lonely woman, living a small, sad life in her childhood bedroom.

Eric used to be proud of his strength and fitness. Panic disorder has changed that. He has gained weight and lost strength since he stopped working out. His old clothes no longer fit. Most days he shuffles around the house in pajama pants, feeling ashamed of his sloppy appearance. Because Eric lacks the confidence to care for his daughter, his mother has started sleeping over when his wife works night shifts. He feels humiliated and inadequate.

What Other Disorders Can Cause Panic Attacks?

Although panic attacks are a defining feature of panic disorder, they are not unique to panic disorder. Panic attacks play a role in many disorders, from phobias to post-traumatic stress disorder.

Ordinary social situations can trigger panic attacks for people with social anxiety. Something as simple as checking out at a store can become unbearable.

Only unexpected panic attacks count as a symptom of panic disorder. Panic attacks related to specific fears may be a sign of a related disorder.

Specific phobias involve an intense fear of a particular object or situation. Common fears include heights, flying, animals, insects, storms, blood, and confined spaces. People with phobias go to great lengths to avoid the things they fear. When they cannot, they may cry, scream, freeze, cling to people, or panic. For example, a man who fears mice may avoid pet stores, grassy areas, and nature documentaries. If he spies a mouse dashing across his living room, he may have a full-blown panic attack.

Most people feel nervous about giving speeches or meeting new people. First dates often feel awkward, and job interviews are stress provoking. Feeling anxious about making a good impression is part of being human. But for people with social anxiety, ordinary social situations feel overwhelming. Routine conversations flood them with fears of humiliating themselves or offending someone. They feel painfully self-conscious and fear rejection. People with social anxiety often manage those fears by withdrawing. They may avoid dating, giving presentations, and taking jobs that require talking to people. They may avoid eating in public or using a public restroom.

When people with social anxiety cannot avoid feared situations, they may have panic attacks. For example, on the way to a job interview, a woman may have intrusive thoughts of stumbling over her words, sweating, and shaking. She imagines the interviewer laughing about her with coworkers afterward. These visions trigger a panic attack, complete with a pounding heart, dizziness, and nausea.

Scott Stossel is a wildly successful author and journalist. His work has appeared in major publications, and he is the editor of the *Atlantic*, a prestigious magazine. Nevertheless, he suffers from serious social anxiety. He writes, "I've frozen, mortifyingly, onstage at public lectures and presentations, and on several occasions I have been compelled to run offstage. I've abandoned dates,

> "I've frozen, mortifyingly, onstage at public lectures and presentations, and on several occasions I have been compelled to run offstage. I've abandoned dates, walked out of exams, and had breakdowns during job interviews."[21]
>
> —Scott Stossel, author

walked out of exams, and had breakdowns during job interviews. . . . In these instances, I have sometimes been convinced that death, or something somehow worse, was imminent."[21]

Separation anxiety involves excessive distress about being away from home or loved ones. Children with separation anxiety may worry constantly about being kidnapped or getting lost. Routine separations, like going to school, produce fears that they will never see their family again. They may have panic attacks if they are forced to go to school or sleep in their own room. Adults with separation anxiety often have unreasonable fears about family members getting sick or hurt. Visions of a deadly roadside accident may cause them to panic when loved ones are running late.

Survivors of life-threatening events may develop post-traumatic stress disorder (PTSD). Assaults, accidents, natural disasters, and wars can all trigger PTSD. Despite attempts to avoid reminders of the trauma, people with PTSD cannot escape it. They re-experience the trauma through intrusive thoughts, nightmares, or flashbacks. People, places, or sensations that remind them of traumatic events may cause panic attacks. A combat veteran may have a panic attack when firecrackers remind her of gunfire. A man who survived a terrible car accident may panic when he hears brakes squealing.

Amanda Wilson, who has PTSD and social anxiety, described how a simple shopping trip drove her to panic. Holiday crowds meant that scooping up a few items took her over an hour. The store was chaotic, with loud music, blaring announcements, and bickering customers. She writes that when she finally reached the checkout line, "my hands were trembling and my lungs were restricting. . . . By this point, the fear was all-consuming. Sweat was rolling down my spine, my lungs were burning, tears were threatening to fall down my face and I was gritting my teeth hard to keep myself from either screaming or crying, trying to quell the nerves that were screaming at me, *run!*"[22]

How Does Panic Disorder Overlap with Other Anxiety Disorders?

Having panic disorder does not protect people against other anxiety disorders. Anxiety disorders are not "separate 'diseases' that one can 'catch' or develop like a common cold and the flu," explains psychologist Rudolph Hatfield.[23] Because anxiety disorders have similar causes, people often have more than one disorder.

Although panic attacks are new for Makayla, anxiety is old news. Until third grade, she cried when her mom dropped her off at school. She had constant stomachaches caused by visions of her mom having a car accident or getting kidnapped. Her parents never had date nights because Makayla would cry for hours if they tried to leave her with a babysitter. Fears of separation weren't Makayla's only problem. As a child, she worried about everything. Tests kept her up all night studying and fretting. Headaches made her worry about brain tumors. A friend turning down a play date made her fear the friendship was over.

Makayla's experience is not unique. Approximately two out of every three people with panic disorder have at least one other anxiety disorder at some point. The majority of people who have both panic disorder and agoraphobia will have another anxiety disorder. Panic disorder overlaps most often with agoraphobia, specific phobia, and social anxiety. Panic disorder is also strongly linked to generalized anxiety disorder (GAD). People with GAD worry too much about school, work, money, friendships, and health. They often feel keyed up, tense, irritable, and tired. Worry makes it tough for them to concentrate or get enough sleep. Approximately one out of every five people with panic disorder also has GAD.

Specific phobias, social phobias, and separation anxiety often develop during the childhood years. Social anxiety often begins in the teen years, an age when everyone becomes more self-conscious. Because panic disorder tends to develop during the late teen or early adult years, people often develop other anxiety disorders first.

Having multiple anxiety disorders is worse than having panic disorder alone. Fortunately, similar treatments work for many anxiety disorders. Medications or talk therapies for panic disorder can reduce symptoms of other anxiety disorders.

What Other Disorders May Happen Along with Panic Disorders?

In addition to anxiety disorders, people with panic disorder are at high risk for a range of other problems. Some of the most common are depression, suicidal thoughts and actions, and substance abuse.

People with panic disorder have a tendency to develop other anxiety disorders. These disorders can cause an overactive response to everyday events and fears.

Just as anxiety disorders involve more than worrying a lot, depression involves much more than feeling sad. A diagnosis of major depression requires intense sadness, irritability, or lack of pleasure lasting at least two weeks. The diagnosis also requires changes in appetite, sleep, energy, self-worth, concentration, or thinking.

Up to two of every three people with panic disorder will have major depression at some point. The high overlap may occur partly because panic and depression share common risk factors. The devastating effects of panic disorder on people's lives may also contribute to depression. Unfortunately, the combination of panic and depression puts people at high risk for suicidal thoughts and actions.

Depression also makes panic disorder harder to treat. Finding a therapist and following a treatment plan is hard work under the best of circumstances. People with depression feel exhausted, hopeless, and helpless. "These feelings of helplessness or hopelessness can interfere with the person's desire or motivation to seek help for their panic attacks and panic disorder," writes Hatfield.[24] Fortunately, depression is treatable. As depression lifts, panic attacks may feel more manageable.

Approximately eight in ten people with panic disorder will have problems with drugs or alcohol at some point in their lives. Many people with agoraphobia develop a drug or alcohol problem. Men with panic disorder face a higher risk of substance use problems than women with panic disorder.

In most cases, problematic substance use develops after panic attacks. People may overuse alcohol, illegal drugs, or prescription drugs in an attempt to self-medicate. Unfortunately, this often backfires. Over time, people need to drink more alcohol or take more drugs to get the same effect. Intoxication and withdrawal can trigger panic attacks. Substance abuse creates a new set of problems.

Depression and substance use have both become problems for Eric. In the past, he handled stress by going on a long run. Since he no longer has that option, he has started drinking throughout the day. He and his wife argue frequently about how drinking affects his parenting.

Eric figures he might as well drink. He takes no pleasure in anything anymore, not even his daughter. He feels physically drained and can't sleep. His constant sadness makes him feel helpless to change his condition and hopeless about the future. Fortunately, Eric is wrong about the potential for change. There are therapies available for all of the problems he faces.

Chapter 3

WHAT ARE RISK FACTORS FOR PANIC DISORDER?

Everyone experiences anxiety, but most people do not have panic attacks. Of those who do have panic attacks, most do not develop panic disorder. What makes the difference? There are biological, environmental, and personal factors that increase risk. Mental health professionals use a variety of techniques to diagnose panic disorder.

What Causes Mental Disorders?

Some medical conditions have an identifiable cause. For example, rhinoviruses cause colds; without the virus, people will not get sick.

But even for such a simple illness, understanding who will get sick is complicated. Some people exposed to the virus fight it off. Others get a minor case of the sniffles. But some people get seriously ill and end up with pneumonia. Doctors cannot predict exactly who will fall into each group.

Predicting who will develop a mental disorder is even more complicated. So is understanding why a specific person develops a specific disorder. Often, that is because there is no one single reason. Psychological problems do not have a clear cause, like a virus. Developing a disorder involves a combination of factors, like biological vulnerability plus intense stress.

Because mental disorders do not have a single cause, researchers study risk factors. They look for the range of biological factors and life experiences that make people vulnerable. This information leads to new ways to prevent and treat disorders.

What Are Biological Risk Factors?

Everyone has biological vulnerabilities. Under enough strain, we will all develop physical or mental problems. Our biology shapes what those problems will be. Some people get migraines; others get stomachaches. Some people become irritable; others have panic attacks. Many different biological factors increase risk for anxiety disorders in general and panic disorder in particular.

Our brains and bodies have a complex fear response system designed to protect us from danger. This fear response system involves many interactive elements. Some brain systems scan the environment for threats. Others sound the alarm, leading to the release of stress hormones. These chemical messengers trigger the body's fight-or-flight response. Still other brain systems handle decisions about how to react to danger, like whether to fight or run.

Some people have brains and bodies tuned to a higher level of threat awareness. People wired with a highly sensitive fear response system react more intensely to threat. They also recover more slowly. Debra Kissen writes, "The brain is always scanning for danger. Sometimes it misfires and determines one is in danger when one is actually safe and sound. A panic attack is simply a false alarm going off in your brain."[25]

Having an active fear response system leads people to experience more worry and anxiety in general. It also keeps people closer to the tipping point at which anxiety becomes full-blown fear. Their active fear response system leads to more false alarms.

> "The brain is always scanning for danger. Sometimes it misfires and determines one is in danger when one is actually safe and sound. A panic attack is simply a false alarm going off in your brain."[25]
>
> —Debra Kissen, psychologist

Communication between brain systems produces our thoughts, feelings, and perceptions. Nerve cells called neurons serve as the wiring for these brain systems. However, neurons cannot pass messages directly to each other because they do not touch. There is a gap between them, called a synapse. When a neuron fires, it releases chemical messengers, called neurotransmitters, into the synapses. Some neurotransmitters excite neurons, making them more likely to fire. Others inhibit neurons, making them less likely to fire.

Each person has a unique brain chemistry. People may release high or low levels of a neurotransmitter or have an especially strong or weak response to it. Differences in brain chemistry can influence the fear response system. Scientists have linked several neurotransmitters to anxiety and panic:

- GABA calms neural activity in brain regions responsible for anxiety and fear.

- Serotonin helps regulate anxiety and sadness.

- Norepinephrine and epinephrine (also known as adrenaline) manage the fight-or-flight reaction. Chemical changes can cause more intense reactions to stress. They can also make people feel tense and anxious.

Medications for panic disorder work by changing the activity of these neurotransmitters in the brain. Some companies sell GABA supplements as an anxiety remedy. Although that seems like a great idea, our bodies are complicated. Swallowing GABA does not change brain levels of GABA.

Another biological factor in anxiety is breathing. Some people tend to take rapid, shallow breaths, especially when anxious. This breathing pattern, called hyperventilation, reduces the amount of carbon dioxide in the bloodstream. Although this change is harmless, the body interprets it as a problem. The heart beats faster and limbs tingle. Blood vessels in the brain constrict, leading to dizziness and disorientation. These panic-like symptoms can lead to panic attacks.

Have you ever held your breath until you truly can't stop yourself from gasping for air? Our bodies have a suffocation alarm that drives us to breathe. Some people have an overly reactive suffocation monitoring system. False alarms produce the terrifying sensation of choking or suffocating when people actually have plenty of air. A faulty suffocation alarm seems to be a key panic attack trigger for some people.

Anxiety and panic disorder tend to run in families. Of course, that could happen for many reasons. Anxious parents may accidentally teach their children to be fearful. Families living in tough situations may all be anxious because they face real threats.

But panic also might run in families because parents pass genetic risks to their children. Genes provide the basic blueprints for our growth and development. They influence brain structure and body chemistry. A child may inherit a tendency to react strongly to stress, along with inheriting her mother's freckles and her father's curly hair.

Research reveals that genes do influence risk for anxiety and panic. However, there is no one panic disorder gene. Instead, many genes play a role. Some genes make people more anxious in general. Others make the body's suffocation alarm more sensitive or strengthen the fight-or-flight response. Some genes seem to increase risk only when combined with stress.

Think about the words you use to describe your friends. Perhaps they are cheerful, kind, energetic, or determined. Those descriptions offer some insight into their personality traits. Personality is complex; your best friend may be generous but quick-tempered. We all have multiple personality traits. Everyone falls somewhere on the spectrums from flaky to reliable, rude to considerate, and quiet to outgoing. Life experiences shape our personality, but biology provides the foundation.

People's personalities interact with their biology. These factors combine to influence their risk of panic disorder.

One personality trait in particular creates a powerful risk for anxiety disorders. Neuroticism involves extra sensitivity to stress and a tendency to feel strong negative emotions. People low in neuroticism are generally calm and even-tempered. People high in neuroticism tend to feel tense and get overwhelmed easily. Often, their intense reaction can make stressful situations even worse.

Not surprisingly, neuroticism strongly predicts anxiety disorders, including panic disorder and agoraphobia. Researchers can even predict the risk of panic disorder in young adults from their emotional reactivity as three-year-olds.

Panic disorder can cause people to assume every physical symptom is a life-threatening problem. They may fear a catastrophic cause behind each pain or ache.

What Lifestyle Factors Increase Risk of Panic Disorders?

Have you ever noticed that juggling too much work makes you more likely to get sick? Or that feeling stressed makes you more anxious and irritable in general? Stress plays a major role in the development of many physical and mental problems. Risk for everything from heart attacks to depression goes up when people get slammed by stress.

People often have their first panic attack during a stressful period. Stress also makes panic attacks more frequent. Psychologist Joanna Arch and colleagues explain, "Stressful life events may elevate levels of anxiety, particularly in vulnerable individuals, which in turn increases the risk for panic."[26] To make matters worse, the fallout from panic attacks often generates more stress. Missing work creates money problems. Skipping school leads to bad grades.

Events from the distant past can also increase a person's risk for panic disorder. Early childhood stress, such as poverty, abuse, and neglect, can permanently alter a person's biology. The more stressful events a person has faced, the greater their risk will be. Although childhood stress increases risk for all disorders, some stressors have an especially close link to panic disorder.

Losing a loved one through separation or death makes panic disorder more likely. Childhood experiences with illness also seem to prime people to develop panic disorder. Having a serious illness or watching a loved one suffer may make people more fearful of physical symptoms. People who have faced illness may be more likely to interpret panic attack symptoms as life-threatening.

Think about the countless upsets you faced as a child. From scraped knees to classmates who won't share the crayons, children deal with problems every day. Parents shape how children learn to think about those experiences. When a child falls while playing tag, what message do they get? Some parents offer a quick hug and encourage their child to get back to the game. Some parents tell their child that running is dangerous and whisk them indoors. Some parents ignore their crying child entirely. Repeating those reactions thousands of times over the course of childhood will influence how children see themselves and the world.

Both overprotective and unresponsive parenting boost risk for panic disorder. Anxious parents tend to produce anxious children. Attempts to keep their children safe lead them to be overprotective

Mental Health Professionals

Many types of mental health professionals have similar sounding names, like psychiatrist, psychologist, and psychotherapist. Although they all start with "psych," these professionals have very different training.

- Psychiatrists are medical doctors who specialize in treating mental disorders. Most focus on prescribing medication rather than providing talk therapy. Other medical doctors can prescribe medication for mental disorders. However, psychiatrists have several extra years of mental health training. Their expertise helps them make diagnoses and identify the right medication for each individual.

- Clinical psychologists have a doctoral degree, which involves four or more years of study after college. They use talk therapy to treat mental disorders. Psychologists with a PhD do independent research during their graduate training. Many make research a central part of their career. Psychologists with a doctor of psychology (PsyD) degree focus on clinical work during their training.

- *Psychotherapist* is a broad term referring to all mental health professionals. However, the term is not restricted. In most states, anyone can call themselves a psychotherapist even if they have no training. People should choose clinicians who have graduate training and are licensed by their state. A license guarantees a basic level of competence and ethical conduct.

There are many other types of mental health professionals, such as counselors and social workers. Most have master's degrees, involving two years of study after college. Typically, they help people manage life problems, such as job loss or domestic violence, rather than treating mental disorders.

and critical. Anxious parents jump in too quickly, solving problems for children instead of letting them learn how to navigate the world. Overprotective parenting can leave children feeling incompetent in a dangerous world.

Unpredictable or unresponsive parenting also contributes to anxiety. Children feel insecure when no one meets their basic needs. They may become clingy to get the support and attention they need.

Unresponsive parenting leads to children who lack confidence and expect rejection.

The way we think about events shapes how we feel about them. A person's perspective can radically alter their risk for panic disorder. In her self-help guide, Kissen writes, "The main differences between people who have an occasional panic attack and those who meet criteria for panic disorder are how much they fear the experience of panic and how much they alter their life to avoid experiencing panic."[27] Researchers have linked panic disorder to several thought patterns that increase anxiety about panic attacks.

People differ in their degree of attention to physical sensations. Some people feel ravenous when lunch is a bit late. Others accidentally skip meals because they never noticed a growling stomach. People who are highly sensitive to every shift in their heart rate or breathing pattern are more likely to develop panic disorder. Focusing on internal sensations opens the door to worrying about them.

Almost every reason for a pounding heart is normal and harmless—like excitement, physical activity, or drinking an energy drink. However, people with panic disorder jump to frightening conclusions. Their pounding heart leads them to think, "I'm having a heart attack." People with panic disorder are prone to anxious interpretations of all physical symptoms. Headaches suggest brain tumors; stomachaches mean an ulcer. As Kissen explains, these people "may be seeing the world through 'panic-colored glasses.' When wearing panic-colored glasses, everything appears dangerous and threatening."[28]

Sensitivity to physical sensations plus catastrophic interpretations is a recipe for panic. Psychologist Edmund Bourne explains, "If you tell yourself that your physiological symptoms are horrible and very threatening, you can't stand them, you're going to lose control, or you might die, you will scare yourself into a very high state of anxiety."[29]

President Franklin D. Roosevelt once said, "the only thing we have to fear is fear itself—nameless, unreasoning, unjustified terror which paralyzes needed efforts to convert retreat into advance."[30] Although he was talking about the Great Depression, the statement applies to panic disorder as well. Many people with panic disorder develop a fear of their fear response. They worry that panic attacks will damage their brain or body. They worry about rejection if someone sees them sweat or tremble. Of course, those worries just amplify anxiety further.

Thoughts have the power to trigger panic attacks. Fortunately, that power can also be harnessed to prevent panic. In fact, Bourne explains, "eliminating catastrophic interpretations of bodily symptoms can, *in and of itself*, be sufficient to relieve panic attacks."[31]

> "Eliminating catastrophic interpretations of bodily symptoms can, *in and of itself*, be sufficient to relieve panic attacks."[31]
>
> —Edmund Bourne, psychologist

How Do These Factors Combine to Cause Panic Attacks?

Panic disorder is not caused by any one thing. Biological vulnerabilities set the stage. Stress activates those vulnerabilities. Then thinking patterns shape how people respond. For most people, the path to developing panic disorder requires a perfect storm of circumstances.

Bourne explains, "You may live twenty years with a hereditary vulnerability to panic attacks and yet never have one. Then life events in your twenties might produce enough cumulative stress to activate what had been only a potential—and you have your first panic attack. If you grew up feeling insecure and were taught that the outside world is dangerous, you may go on to develop agoraphobia."[32]

> "You may live twenty years with a hereditary vulnerability to panic attacks and yet never have one. Then life events in your twenties might produce enough cumulative stress to activate what had been only a potential—and you have your first panic attack."[32]
>
> —Edmund Bourne, psychologist

Eric and Makayla were both born with some biological risk factors. Eric had an easily triggered fight-or-flight response. Makayla had an anxious personality. Makayla's parents reacted to her worries with overprotection. Their concern made her doubt her ability to solve problems and taught her to retreat from things she feared.

Both Eric and Makayla monitored their bodies constantly and responded to changes with catastrophic thinking. Normal sensations, like feeling sweaty on a summer day, would convince Eric an episode was coming. A hint of a dizziness would make Makayla certain she was about to go insane.

Having multiple panic attacks eventually teaches some people that panic attacks are harmless. Instead, Eric and Makayla both developed an intense fear of panic attacks. Eric believed that each episode caused lasting damage to his heart. Makayla felt sure her terror would cause her mind to snap.

Fortunately, both Makayla and Eric got help. When it became clear that Makayla was getting worse, her mom arranged for her to see a psychiatrist. At the urging of his wife, Eric agreed to meet with a psychologist. Different types of doctors can help in different ways.

How Do Doctors Diagnose Panic Disorder?

For Eric's psychologist to help him, she will need to accurately diagnose his panic disorder, agoraphobia, excessive alcohol use, and growing depression. Diagnosis will be complicated because Eric doesn't yet have any insight into those problems. He keeps rushing to the emergency room because he believes he has a rare heart problem.

Diagnosing panic disorder is challenging. Many medical problems produce panic-like symptoms. Panic attacks occur across many different mental disorders. Although approximately eight in ten people with panic disorder seek help, fewer than five in ten get help that meets treatment guidelines. One reason is that many people look for help in the wrong place. Psychiatrist Borwin Bandelow writes, "Patients with panic disorder often assume that they

"Patients with panic disorder often assume that they have a medical rather than a psychiatric condition and tend to have themselves re-examined repeatedly in internal medical or emergency wards."[33]

—Borwin Bandelow, psychiatrist

Therapists may go on trips with their clients to see how the client responds to frightening situations, such as a crowded theater. This can help a therapist guide the client's treatment plan.

have a medical rather than a psychiatric condition and tend to have themselves re-examined repeatedly in internal medical or emergency wards."[33] Mental health professionals are better prepared to diagnose panic disorder. To do so, they use a combination of interviews, questionnaires, and observations.

Heart problems, hormone imbalances, and seizures can all cause panic-like events. Asthma, allergies, migraines, and low blood sugar can also produce symptoms that mimic panic disorder. Drugs and medications can also cause panic-like symptoms. Caffeine, decongestants, blood-pressure medications, steroids, and recreational drugs are common culprits. They can speed heart rate or make people feel dizzy and disconnected from reality.

Ruling out medical problems is a crucial step in diagnosing panic disorder. Psychiatrists can do the exam themselves. Psychologists may refer clients to medical doctors. Often, by the time someone with panic disorder sees a therapist, they have had many physical exams.

To diagnose panic disorder, clinicians interview clients about their symptoms. Many clinicians use structured interviews to make sure they capture all essential information. These interviews include detailed questions about every symptom. For example, the Mini International Neuropsychiatric Interview (MINI) starts with a broad question: "Have you, on more than one occasion, had spells or attacks when you suddenly felt anxious, frightened, uncomfortable or uneasy, even in situations where most people would not feel that way?" If the answer is yes, the MINI guides the clinician to get more details. Follow up questions include, "Did you have skipping, racing or pounding of your heart?" and "Did you fear that you were dying?"[34] During the interview, clinicians also explore other possible explanations for panic attacks. It makes no sense to treat someone for panic disorder if they actually have social anxiety.

Scores on questionnaires give clinicians a sense of the severity of a person's symptoms. Clinicians can choose from many different questionnaires. Some measure anxiety in general; others assess specific panic symptoms. Questionnaires may also dive deeply into specific thoughts and behaviors. For example, behavior-change scales ask clients about specific situations they avoid. Anxiety-sensitivity scales measure fear of panic symptoms and social judgment.

Some clinicians use trips to feared places as part of the assessment. These observations offer valuable insight into how clients manage fear.

Studying Panic Attacks in the Lab

For a researcher studying panic, the ideal situation is to be with people during attacks. That helps capture details about their thoughts, feelings, and physical reactions. However, panic attacks are unpredictable. To get around this problem, some researchers ask brave volunteers to endure panic attacks in the lab.

Scientists can trigger panic attacks by administering drugs or changing body chemistry. One common approach involves having people inhale extra carbon dioxide. Because carbon dioxide builds up when people cannot breathe, inhaling it can trigger the body's suffocation alarm. Almost everyone who breathes in extra carbon dioxide feels dizzy and tingly and has their heart beat faster. For people vulnerable to panic, carbon dioxide often produces a panic attack.

Researchers have used this trigger to test the effect of medications and exercise on panic attacks. They have also used it to explore the impact of thoughts on panic. For example, placing medical rescue gear in the room makes people who fear heart disease more likely to panic. The equipment seems to activate their fears of having a heart attack, causing them to react more strongly to the carbon dioxide.

This type of research asks a lot of the participants. Scientists have an ethical obligation to make sure people know what the study involves. Although panic attacks are miserable, many people are willing to suffer to advance treatment for everyone.

Therapists often have clients record details about each panic attack. Clients will note the time, place, and length of each attack. They may also rate the severity of each panic symptom and record anxious thoughts.

For many people, getting an accurate diagnosis is a relief. People realize they are not in danger. Getting an accurate diagnosis is also the first step toward effective treatment. Doctors and other specialists use a range of medications and therapies to treat panic disorder.

Chapter 4

HOW IS PANIC DISORDER TREATED?

Although almost everyone with panic disorder seeks help, many never get the most effective treatments. Because not all treatments are equally helpful, people may suffer unnecessarily. Researchers have tested many options to identify treatments that work. Cognitive behavioral therapy, mindful acceptance, and certain medications all have good track records. Not every treatment works for every person, but these evidence-based treatments offer the best chance of success.

What Is Talk Therapy?

Many mental health professionals treat panic disorder using talk therapy, also called psychotherapy. Talk therapy usually involves

Therapy can help people develop skills to manage panic disorder. Mental health professionals are trained to listen to patients' concerns and give useful advice.

weekly meetings lasting approximately an hour. Therapists may schedule longer sessions to help clients tackle a feared situation.

Psychologists John Forsyth and Georg Eifert compare therapy to learning to ride a bike. They write, "The only way to learn how to ride a bike is to get on one and start riding. You also need to be willing to fall once in a while, because you will. There's no other way to learn. It takes practice, commitment to learning how to do it, willingness to experience pain and falls, and recommitment to getting back on the bike after a fall."[35] Therapy works the same way. People need to learn new skills and practice them between sessions. Sometimes that practice will feel hard. But therapists are coaches, not miracle workers. To succeed, people will need to make changes.

In therapy, people often talk about thoughts and feelings they have never shared with anyone. Therapists have a legal and ethical obligation to keep that information private. With adult clients, therapists can only break confidentiality to prevent harm. For example, they may report abuse or suicidality.

Confidentiality is more complicated for children because parents have a right to their medical records. Therapists usually work out agreements with parents to share only essential information. For example, a therapist might describe skills covered during a session but leave out details about a child's thoughts and feelings.

Although there are many approaches to treating panic disorder, they all share similar goals. Common treatment goals are reducing the frequency and severity of panic attacks, minimizing the places and activities people avoid, and getting people back to regular activities.

What Is Cognitive Behavioral Therapy?

If you have ever tried to stop feeling sad, mad, or scared, you know it is virtually impossible to change your feelings directly. However, people can make choices about how they think and act. Similarly, people with panic disorder cannot turn off their fear. However, they can change how they think about panic attacks. They can behave differently when panic strikes. Over time, changing these thoughts and actions will make panic less overwhelming.

Cognitive behavioral therapy (CBT) is based on the idea that changing thoughts and behaviors will change how a person feels. It is the best-supported talk therapy for panic and agoraphobia. CBT for panic has many elements, all directed toward helping people face fears directly.

Therapists begin by explaining the causes of panic attacks and panic disorder. Treatment guidelines from the American Psychiatric Association explain the importance of this step: "Education alone may relieve some of the symptoms of panic disorder by helping the patient realize that his or her symptoms are neither life-threatening nor uncommon."[36] Knowing what is happening makes panic attacks less frightening. Learning about biological elements helps people see that panic has nothing to do with their willpower or character.

When anxious people take rapid, shallow breaths, it changes their body chemistry. Hyperventilation leads to panic symptoms like dizziness, tingling, a racing heart, and disorientation. Therapists teach breathing exercises to reverse that process. Psychologist Debra Kissen writes, "The most powerful technique to calm down your body is slow breathing. . . . All you need to do, to take the wind out of the sails of a brewing panic attack, is to engage in five minutes of slow breathing. By engaging in slow, deep breathing, you will send the signal to your brain 'the coast is clear; we are not in danger.'"[37] When people feel calmer, they are better able to use the other tools they learn in therapy.

"In a calm, panic-free moment, it is easy to understand that a panic attack is simply a false alarm going off in

> "The most powerful technique to calm down your body is slow breathing. . . . All you need to do, to take the wind out of the sails of a brewing panic attack, is to engage in five minutes of slow breathing. By engaging in slow, deep breathing, you will send the signal to your brain 'the coast is clear; we are not in danger.'"[37]
>
> —Debra Kissen, psychologist

your brain and you need not fear it," says Kissen. "But in the midst of a panic attack, it is hard to think rationally."[38] A major element of CBT is learning to recognize and challenge unrealistic fears. Therapists help clients recognize that scary thoughts can feel true without being true.

People with panic disorder work hard to avoid panic-like sensations. CBT therapists reverse that strategy, encouraging clients to create uncomfortable sensations intentionally. Clients may spin in a chair to get dizzy and nauseous. They may breathe through a straw to feel suffocated. Sitting with these sensations teaches clients that the feelings are tolerable and harmless. This practice, called interoceptive exposure, helps break the link between minor physical symptoms and full-blown panic attacks. Kissen explains, "The more short-term discomfort you let yourself experience, the more long-term peace you will obtain."[39]

After the panic attacks became more frequent, Eric avoided all physical exertion. He hated being hot, sweaty, or out of breath. Feeling his heart speed up terrified him. His therapist had him tackle each of these sensations.

"The more short-term discomfort you let yourself experience, the more long-term peace you will obtain."[39]

—Debra Kissen, psychologist

To get used to having his heart beat faster, Eric started by walking briskly. Once he could tolerate that feeling without panicking, he started doing pushups. At first, he could only handle a few pushups at a time. But within two weeks, Eric could do 20 pushups without getting scared by his pounding heart. Eric started exercising again, which made him feel more energetic and less stressed. These sessions also gave Eric a chance to practice realistic thinking skills. Just like sports drills prepare athletes for games, these exposure sessions prepared Eric to cope when panic hit.

Therapists also have clients practice going to places they have been avoiding. This practice is known as exposure therapy. Clients may practice driving over bridges or visiting crowded shopping centers. They may take a center seat in a packed movie theater or board a bus during rush hour. As part of this exposure therapy, clients also eliminate safety behaviors. They go out alone instead of bringing a friend. They leave their medication at home. Leaving safety items behind shows people that they can face tough situations independently.

In her self-help manual, Kissen sums up the essence of exposure therapy: "A no-fail way to put panic in its place and show it that you are the boss of your own life is to always do the opposite of what panic asks of you! If it tells you to avoid something, you should go, go, go! If it tells you not to do something because it may bring on scary sensations, purposely do it!"[40]

CBT helps most people. Approximately 70 to 80 percent of people who complete CBT end up panic-free. People can also beat panic disorder even if they still have panic attacks. They can learn to see panic as an annoyance rather than a terrifying event.

What Is Acceptance and Commitment Therapy?

Panic attacks are exhausting and unpleasant. No one wants to endure them. However, panic attacks are not the sole cause of panic disorder. Panic disorder comes from people's desperate attempts to avoid unpleasant thoughts and feelings. Psychologists Forsyth and Eifert explain that anxiety itself is not the problem. Instead, they say, "the struggle with our minds and bodies is the root cause of human suffering. . . . Perhaps the struggle is unnecessary and even part of the problem with anxiety."[41]

Acceptance and commitment therapy (ACT) helps people develop a new perspective on anxiety and panic. Like CBT, ACT encourages people to face feelings and experiences directly rather than avoiding them. Unlike CBT, ACT therapists do not encourage clients to challenge negative thoughts. Instead, ACT therapists teach mindful awareness. Instead of debating anxious thoughts or trying to push them away, clients simply notice them with curiosity. ACT and other therapies focused on mindful acceptance of feelings help reduce symptoms of panic and agoraphobia.

"Resisting or fleeing symptoms of anxiety tends to make them worse," write Forsyth and Eifert. "The more you can adopt an attitude of acceptance, no matter how unpleasant the symptoms may be, the better your ability to cope will be."[42] Clients do not need to engage with upsetting thoughts. They can simply observe them and allow them to pass.

Everyone feels physical and emotional pain sometimes. Eliminating all anxiety is simply not a reasonable goal. However, we can still be happy despite unwanted thoughts and feelings. ACT therapists suggest giving up the losing battle to avoid pain. Instead, they believe we should focus on identifying our values and building a rich and meaningful life. Kissen writes, "To fully reclaim your life, you must try to do things that you value despite panic sensations occasionally surfacing. When you live fully, you experience life as meaningful despite moments of discomfort."[43]

Based on the advice of her psychiatrist, Makayla met weekly with an ACT therapist. Together, they identified Makayla's strategies for avoiding anxiety. Some were obvious, like skipping school. Other strategies were more subtle. For example, whenever a scary thought popped into her head, Makayla would play loud music or check social media.

> "To fully reclaim your life, you must try to do things that you value despite panic sensations occasionally surfacing. When you live fully, you experience life as meaningful despite moments of discomfort."[43]
>
> —Debra Kissen, psychologist

Makayla's therapist had her practice a new approach. Instead of trying to make scary thoughts go away, Makayla focused on them directly. She stopped trying to block thoughts like, "I'm going insane." She just noticed those thoughts as they came and went, like storm clouds passing through the sky.

Similarly, when Makayla had dizzy spells, she purposefully shifted her attention to the sensations. She would observe the pattern of tingly feelings or notice how the tightness of her chest shifted with each breath. At first, Makayla expected this to make dizzy spells even more overwhelming. To her surprise, mindful awareness made even the scariest sensations less powerful. Makayla discovered that moving into observer mode kept her from being swept away in a flood of panicky thoughts and feelings. Once fear held less power over her, Makayla was able to put her energy into things she loved. After just a

A person with agoraphobia might ride a crowded bus as part of exposure therapy. This can help them get used to crowds and can gradually lessen their anxiety over time.

few weeks, she was back to playing soccer and spending time with friends.

What Medications Are Available for Panic Disorder?

Medications for panic disorder can be used alone or combined with talk therapy. Several different categories of medication can help.

Each type has distinct pros and cons. People may have to try different types to find one that works well for them.

Benzodiazepines are relaxants that reduce panic attacks and overall anxiety. They work by making more of the neurotransmitter GABA available. GABA slows down brain activity, producing a calming effect. Commonly prescribed brands include Ativan and Xanax.

Benzodiazepines can be taken daily to keep anxiety levels low. Because benzodiazepines are fast acting, people can also take them only when they feel especially anxious. The major downside is that benzodiazepines can be addictive. With regular use, people might develop a tolerance, needing more of the drug to get the same effect. Common side effects include memory issues, drowsiness, dizziness, confusion, and poor coordination. People may not be able to drive safely. These concerns may lead patients to stop taking their medicines without telling a doctor. Depending on the dose, this could backfire. People might be more anxious when they stop taking the medicine than they were before they started.

Several different types of antidepressants can reduce depression, anxiety, and panic attacks. For panic, doctors usually choose selective serotonin reuptake inhibitors (SSRIs) because they have the fewest side effects. Commonly prescribed brands include Paxil, Prozac, and Zoloft.

SSRIs work by making more of the neurotransmitter serotonin available. When some neurons fire, they release serotonin to communicate with surrounding neurons. That serotonin is usually immediately cleared from the gap between neurons. SSRIs slow that

How Do We Know What Works?

To treat panic disorder, clinicians do not just make their best guess about what works. Doing that would be dangerous. People are great at tricking themselves into thinking that useless treatments help. This process is known as the placebo effect. Studies have found that people's expectations alter outcomes. For example, if people are given a harmless sugar pill for an illness, they may report feeling better afterwards, even though the pill had no effect. The placebo effect is so powerful that people will feel better after almost any treatment. But the placebo effect only lasts for a little while.

Scientists have tested many different treatments for panic disorder. Scientists generally test treatments on a small group before the treatments are released to the general public. Most tests have at least two groups of patients; one group receives the new treatment and the other receives a placebo. Then scientists compare the results from the two groups. If the new treatment shows promise, scientists will keep working on it.

process, leaving more serotonin floating around. Over time, making more serotonin available can desensitize the brain's fear network.

SSRIs have a low addiction potential. However, most people need to take SSRIs every day for weeks before they see a benefit. Side effects tend to emerge before benefits, so people may quit taking SSRIs before seeing any change. The most common side effects are upset stomach, headaches, dizziness, and weight gain.

Beta-blockers are used mainly to treat high blood pressure and heart conditions. These medications interfere with the fight-or-flight response by blocking the effects of adrenaline. Beta-blockers can reduce physical symptoms of anxiety, like having a pounding heart, sweating, or feeling jittery. However, beta blockers do not reduce anxiety in general. Doctors rarely choose them as the main treatment for panic disorder. Side effects include fatigue, weight gain, and cold hands and feet.

What Steps Can People Take Themselves?

Professional treatment can be costly and time-consuming. It may not even be an option for people who do not live near qualified providers. Self-help may work for milder cases of panic disorder or highly motivated clients. It may be the best option open to people without access to a specialist. Before choosing a self-help approach, people should see a medical doctor to rule out physical health issues.

Common self-help options include workbooks, online communities, and apps. Workbooks based on research-supported therapies, such as ACT and CBT, show promise. For example, people who used an ACT self-help workbook found anxiety less overwhelming. They avoided fewer locations.

Unfortunately, not every self-help resource helps. There are more than 50 smartphone apps for panic. Some offer breathing or mindfulness exercises. Others help people track panic attacks. Most have not been tested in any way. When researchers reviewed these apps, they found that many had inaccurate information or promoted the sale of untested products.

Living a healthy lifestyle is another form of self-help. Exercising, getting enough sleep, and eating a healthy diet helps with most physical and mental problems. Although more research is needed, exercise seems to reduce anxiety in general. Tobacco, alcohol, caffeine, and illegal drugs can all amplify panic symptoms. Minimizing substance use can make panic attacks less likely.

What Are Alternative Treatments for Panic Disorder?

There are many unproven treatments for panic disorder, such as hypnosis, herbal remedies, acupuncture, aromatherapy, and massage. Much of the support for these treatments comes from anecdotes—a story told by one person about how the treatment worked for them. Anecdotes feel like powerful evidence but cannot prove a treatment works. Although people do feel better after alternative treatments, the improvement may have nothing to do with the treatment.

Thanks to the placebo effect, people can get real symptom relief from any treatment they trust. Fake medications, fake acupuncture, and even fake surgeries can make people feel better. The placebo effect is especially powerful for symptoms like pain, nausea, sleep problems, and anxiety.

Fortunately, most alternative treatments are harmless. Whether or not massage treats panic, it feels great. The worst possible outcome is wasted time and money. However, some herbal remedies and supplements can be dangerous. People think *natural* means healthy and pure. But not all natural remedies are safe. Many of the world's deadliest poisons come from plants. Kava, a natural remedy for anxiety, can cause serious illness or death.

The manufacture and sale of natural remedies is not well regulated. Manufacturers do not have to prove their product has a benefit. Products may not even contain the ingredients listed on the label. People should talk to a doctor before taking supplements.

Exercising and getting outdoors can help reduce anxiety.

How Do People Plan Treatment?

Talk therapy and medications can reduce symptoms of both panic disorder and agoraphobia. Clients may choose just one approach, or they may combine therapy and medication. Experts recommend talk therapies that include exposure, such as CBT or ACT.

In the short term, prescribing medications offers the fastest relief. In the long term, providing talk therapy predicts the best outcomes. The benefits of medications disappear once people stop taking them, but gains from talk therapy are long-lasting.

Because medications and talk therapy both help, treatment guidelines encourage providers to consider client preferences.

Medication may be a better option for someone who is too busy for weekly sessions or who lives too far from a psychologist. Drug treatment guidelines suggest prescribing SSRIs first because they have the fewest risks.

Talk therapy may be the best choice for someone who wants or needs to avoid drugs. Medications carry high risks for some people. Children taking benzodiazepines feel groggy and face a higher addiction risk. SSRIs can increase suicidality in children and teens. Elderly people process medications more slowly, leading to stronger side effects. They are also more likely to be taking medications for physical problems. Those medications may react badly with drugs for panic disorder. Therapy alone may be a better first choice for younger and older clients.

Treatment planning for Eric and Makayla considered their symptoms and preferences. Eric was comfortable with the idea of taking medications and eager to get back to work. His psychologist referred him to a doctor, who prescribed SSRIs. Although Makayla was seeing a psychiatrist, her mother hoped to avoid drug treatment. Her psychiatrist helped Makayla find an expert in ACT. Makayla got good results from talk therapy, so she never needed medication.

What Happens after Treatment?

Treatment doesn't magically solve panic disorder. If a person gets stressed, panic attacks may pop back up. The return of panic attacks does not mean that treatment failed. It just means that people need to go back to the approach that worked before. The medications and coping skills that worked the first time will work again. Kissen explains, "It is important to remember that your success is not defined by the presence of panicky thoughts or feelings, but rather by the way that you choose to respond to panicky thoughts and feelings."[44]

Both Eric and Makayla learned to manage panic. Eric worked with a CBT therapist for approximately 16 weeks. After the first month, he was back to work. By the end of his treatment, he no longer avoided any activities. He spent weekends playing with his daughter and hiking with his wife. After about a year, he stopped taking SSRIs. Although Eric's heart still raced occasionally, it no longer scared him.

For Makayla, simply learning about panic disorder helped. Once she understood her strange symptoms, she stopped worrying about going insane. After two therapy sessions, she went back to school. After three months of therapy, she had learned to observe dizzy spells with calm curiosity. She still had odd sensations sometimes, but no longer changed her behavior because of them. Instead of letting fear guide her life, she kept her focus on the things that mattered most to her. Makayla spent time laughing with friends, playing soccer, and applying to colleges. Before treatment, she thought her life was over. Now she feels ready for all the adventures yet to come.

> "It is important to remember that your success is not defined by the presence of panicky thoughts or feelings, but rather by the way that you choose to respond to panicky thoughts and feelings."[44]
>
> —Debra Kissen, psychologist

SOURCE NOTES

INTRODUCTION: A MOMENT OF PANIC

1. Quoted in Sarah Schuster, "What it's Like to Have a Panic Attack, from 24 People Who've Been There," *The Mighty*, September 2, 2015. themighty.com.

2. Stanley Rachman and Padmal de Silva, *Panic Disorder: The Facts*. New York: Oxford UP, 2009, p. 6.

3. American Psychiatric Association, *Diagnostic and Statistical Manual of Mental Disorders*. Arlington, VA: American Psychiatric Publishing, 2013, p. 208.

4. Gordon J.G. Asmundson, Daniel M. LeBouthillier, and Steven Taylor, "Anxiety Disorders: Panic Disorder and Agoraphobia." *Psychiatry*, Chichester, UK: John Wiley & Sons, Ltd., p. 1064.

5. Michael A. Tompkins, *Anxiety and Avoidance: A Universal Treatment for Anxiety, Panic, and Fear*. Oakland, CA: New Harbinger Publications, 2013, p. 12.

CHAPTER 1: WHAT IS PANIC DISORDER?

6. Bret A. Moore, *Taking Control of Anxiety: Small Steps for Getting the Best of Worry, Stress, and Fear*. Washington, DC: American Psychological Association, 2014, p. 7.

7. Bailey Griffin, "To My Friends Who Are Curious about What a Panic Attack Feels Like," *The Mighty*, July 1, 2017. themighty.com.

8. *Diagnostic and Statistical Manual of Mental Disorders*, p. 214.

9. Quoted in Sarah Watts, "11 Women Share What a Panic Attack Really Feels Like," *Women's Health Mag*, July 19, 2017. www.womenshealthmag.com.

10. Rachman and de Silva, *Panic Disorder*, p. 13.

11. *Diagnostic and Statistical Manual of Mental Disorders*, p. 215.

12. *Diagnostic and Statistical Manual of Mental Disorders*, p. 215.

13. Rachman and de Silva, *Panic Disorder*, p. 20.

14. Rachman and de Silva, *Panic Disorder*, p. 12.

15. *Diagnostic and Statistical Manual of Mental Disorders*, p. 219.

CHAPTER 2: WHAT ARE THE EFFECTS OF PANIC DISORDER?

16. Rachman and de Silva, *Panic Disorder*, p. 28.

17. Rita Z. Chin, "Resolve and Resilience from Panic," *Anxiety and Depression Association of America*, n.d. adaa.org.

18. Jennifer Shannon, *The Anxiety Survival Guide for Teens: CBT Skills to Overcome Fear, Worry, and Panic.* Oakland, CA: New Harbinger Publications, 2015, p. 19.

19. Debra Kissen, *The Panic Workbook for Teens: Breaking the Cycle of Fear, Worry, and Panic Attacks.* Oakland, CA: New Harbinger Publications, 2015, p. 158.

20. Kissen, *The Panic Workbook for Teens*, p. 1.

21. Scott Stossel, *My Age of Anxiety: Fear, Hope, Dread, and the Search for Peace of Mind.* New York: Random House, 2013, p. 5–6.

22. Amanda Wilson, "To the Cashier Who Realized I Was Having a Panic Attack," *The Mighty*, December 29, 2016. themighty.com.

23. Rudolph C. Hatfield, *The Everything Guide to Coping With Panic Disorder: Learn How to Take Control of Your Panic and Live a Healthier, Happier Life.* Avon, MA: Avons Media, 2014, p. 114.

24. Hatfield, *The Everything Guide to Coping With Panic Disorder*, p. 111.

CHAPTER 3: WHAT ARE RISK FACTORS FOR PANIC DISORDER?

25. Kissen, *The Panic Workbook for Teens*, p. 30.

26. Joanna J. Arch, Lauren N. Landy, and Michelle G. Craske, "Panic Disorder." *Psychopathology: History, Diagnosis, and Empirical Foundations.* San Francisco, CA: John Wiley & Sons Ltd., 2013, pp. 197, 207.

27. Kissen, *The Panic Workbook for Teens*, p. 34.

28. Kissen, *The Panic Workbook for Teens*, p. 20.

29. Edmund J. Bourne, *The Anxiety and Phobia Workbook*. Oakland, CA: New Harbinger Publications, 2015, p. 146.

30. Quoted in "Only Thing We Have to Fear Is Fear Itself: FDR's First Inaugural Address," *History Matters*, n.d. www.historymatters.gmu.edu.

31. Bourne, *The Anxiety and Phobia Workbook*, p. 132.

32. Bourne, *The Anxiety and Phobia Workbook*, p. 47.

33. Borwin Bandelow and Sophie Michaelis, "Epidemiology of Anxiety Disorders in the 21st Century," *NCBI*, September 2015. www.ncbi.nlm.gov.

34. D. Sheehan, et al., "Mini International Neuropsychiatric Interview," *University of Alabama at Birmingham*, July 1, 2005. www.uab.edu.

CHAPTER 4: HOW IS PANIC DISORDER TREATED?

35. John P. Forsyth and Georg H. Eifert, *The Mindfulness and Acceptance Workbook for Anxiety: A Guide to Breaking Free from Anxiety, Phobias, and Worry Using Acceptance and Commitment Therapy.* Oakland, CA: New Harbinger Publications, 2016, p. 23.

36. "Practice Guideline for the Treatment of Patients with Panic Disorder," *Psychiatry Online*, 2010. psychiatryonline.org.

37. Kissen, *The Panic Workbook for Teens*, p. 115.

38. Kissen, *The Panic Workbook for Teens*, p. 68.

39. Kissen, *The Panic Workbook for Teens*, p. 57.

40. Kissen, *The Panic Workbook for Teens*, p. 147.

41. Forsyth and Eifert, *The Mindfulness and Acceptance Workbook for Anxiety*, p. 9.

42. Bourne, *The Anxiety and Phobia Workbook*, p. 151.

43. Kissen, *The Panic Workbook for Teens*, p. 130.

44. Kissen, *The Panic Workbook for Teens*, p. 135.

BOOKS

Edmund J. Bourne, *The Anxiety and Phobia Workbook*. Oakland, CA: New Harbinger Publications, 2015.

Rudolph C. Hatfield, T*he Everything Guide to Coping with Panic Disorder: Learn How to Take Control of Your Panic and Live a Healthier, Happier Life*. Avon, MA: Adams Media, 2014.

Debra Kissen, *The Panic Workbook for Teens: Breaking the Cycle of Fear, Worry, and Panic Attacks*. Oakland, CA: New Harbinger Publications, 2015.

Bret A. Moore, *Taking Control of Anxiety: Small Steps for Getting the Best of Worry, Stress, and Fear*. Washington, DC: American Psychological Association, 2014.

Jennifer Shannon, *The Anxiety Survival Guide for Teens: CBT Skills to Overcome Fear, Worry, and Panic*. Oakland, CA: New Harbinger Publications, 2015.

INTERNET SOURCES

Barbara J. King, "What Is It Like to Suffer from an Anxiety Disorder?" *NPR*, October 5, 2017. www.npr.org.

Gila Lyons, "When Life Gave Me Lemons, I Had a Panic Attack," *New York Times*, January 24, 2018. www.nytimes.com.

WEBSITES

Anxiety and Depression Association of America
adaa.org

The Anxiety and Depression Association of America works to prevent and treat emotional disorders. Its website describes panic disorder, offers expert tips for managing stress and panic attacks, and helps people find treatment options.

Anxiety.org: Panic Disorder
www.anxiety.org/panic-disorder-panic-attacks

This website offers expert information about panic disorder symptoms, causes, and treatments, as well as information about other anxiety disorders.

Psychiatry.org: Help with Anxiety Disorders
www.psychiatry.org/patients-families/anxiety-disorders

The national organization of psychiatrists runs this website. It offers facts about disorders and treatment options, patient stories, and breaking news. It also helps people find specialists nearby.

Teen Mental Health: Mental Disorders
teenmentalhealth.org/learn/mental-disorders

The Teen Mental Health website describes panic disorder and other common problems. It offers first-hand stories about living with mental health problems and facing stigma. The website also has expert information about managing stress and communicating about problems.

INDEX

IMAGE CREDITS

ABOUT THE AUTHOR

Jennifer Connor-Smith, PhD, is a clinical psychologist. Before shifting her focus to writing, she researched stress and coping, and she trained other therapists to treat anxiety and depression. She has seen more teenagers and adults beat panic disorder than she can count.